CONTENTS

III

I THOUGHT I MISSED HIM

Poetry

I THOUGHT I MISSED HIM

Diana Townsend

CONTENT WARNING

Readers, I appreciate you taking the time to read my poetry. Your mental health matters to me so I want to be clear that this is not happy or sweet poetry. These poems describe the intense feelings that I experienced after toxic break-ups. There will be mention of triggering events such as:

- narcissistic behavior
- cheating
- emotional abuse
- anger issues/violence
- lying
- suicidal thoughts
- toxic relationships

REMNANTS OF HIM

How long before my flesh
forgets the pressure of your body on mine,
before my skin cells renew
and this body
is rid of your kisses and caresses?

I long to be made new
and I pray my brain will follow suit
and forget the day
you smiled at me
and I lost myself in your eyes.

Sticky,
the residue of you…
it lingers on my weathered soul
and I miss you
being an extension of my heart
on loan for the world to enjoy.

Toxic love affairs
tend to expose the weakest versions
of who we are
inside.

My ego humors me
and convinces my brain that you
are sleep deprived
and thinking of me
as well.

I hope that it is true.

But I know it's not.

I called and hung up before you could answer
but of course, you texted right back
asking what I wanted...

I thought I wanted you.
I thought you wanted me.

What a shame.

This boy changed the way
I viewed the world
and while I knew he was mostly wrong
about the ways of the world
playing the devil's advocate felt like more fun
at the time.

Monday, he's blocked
Tuesday, unblocked but no contact
Wednesday, I send a text but
quickly delete the thread
Thursday, I wait to see if it goes
from delivered to read
Friday, I cry at work when it still says delivered...

I would have read your messages.
You know that... deep inside.

Two dreamers
who promised to always be friends
no matter what
but break-ups have a way
of ripping souls apart
and revealing the stab wounds in the back
the ones we so carefully covered
with bright smiles
and good intentions.

Movies, music, candy
these things still taste of you
of what we shared
they reek of the joy
I felt in this space
in this place
when you were still
here.

That sinking feeling
of regret
sneaks up on me in the middle of the night
you were my favorite person
and now we are complete strangers.

I whisper your name
like a secret in the dark
wishing and hoping
that my quiet thoughts
could somehow summon you
home.

Memories are meaningless
when I am in mourning
while you roam the earth
seeking to replace
me.

You left me
but you also left my little sister
my baby brothers
and my mom and dad...

they ask about you often,
but you have not asked about them
once.

Healing sounds so easy
my apps suggest it takes time and hydration
growth and strength
perseverance and no contact...

but I miss you.

I miss us.

I miss who I was when we were together.

I wish I had never checked
your phone
your stories
your timelines

I wish I could delete it all.

You texted me last night
and I read them
over and over
but did not
respond.

No one warned me that our songs
would burn my ears
after you left...
they never told me how your cologne
would stink
on other men...
and I found out the hard way
that your spot
in my bed
was not made
for random lovers.

There aren't enough pillows
to replace your cuddling body
next to mine…
but I make do,
somehow.

Minutes feel like hours when your heart is broken...
yes, that much is true.
But the clock ticks faster when I remember
the sound of your yelling
or your temper tantrums
or your selfish ability to make everything
about you.
Time, it seems, hurts as much as it heals.

People love to preach
that we are whom we attract
but I pray that isn't true.

I pray that is not true.

I once thought the stars aligned
for us to be together
I thought that we crashed into each other
a beautiful wreck
what a sight to see...

Life has shown me
that love should not include
trauma.

I shouldn't have had to survive you.

Friends turned into lovers
and we thought we beat the odds
smug and happy
the obnoxious air of new love...

nothing could have prepared me
for our lovers-to-enemies trope
for I thought we were better than that
better than raised voices and sarcastic remarks
better than heavy hands and clenched fists
oh, I thought we could survive it all.

I thought we would survive it all.

I still hear your lies
in my sleep
mumbled confessions of how you
never meant to hurt me...

but you could never explain
how you accidentally break the heart
of the woman you claim to love
more than life itself.

You should have been more willing
to fall upon your sword
than to see me cry.

I guess I was not worth that.

You wound me up
and I spun like ribbons of sugar
delicate and sweet
dissolving into the descent of your love
drowning in the sticky remnants of lust...

You wound me up
and made me believe in fairy tales
and happy endings
and yet here I am...
alone.

You wound me up.

This empty ache swells
it pushes me to the edge of sanity
and as I tiptoe to peek over
my intrusive thoughts battling my logic
your love was never the reason
I felt fulfilled.

I forgot how freely I roamed this world
before I became
your shadow.

The initial minutes after the breakup
are melancholy...
the agony sets in, and seconds drag on
the ticking of my biological clock
the reset of another talking stage
the frustration of real love
exposed as a fraud.

It is exhausting on the molecular level.

If I text you first,
the moons will collide
the stars will combust
and my heart will crumble into the dust
of the galaxy that was
our love.

If I break no contact before you do,
then I am a failure
a weak minion
and you would know
that I spend hours
checking my phone...
waiting for you
to give in.

Our good days turned into good weeks
all because I chose to
stay quiet.

I stopped speaking about the little things
that bothered me
or caused me to lose sleep
and I learned how to navigate your temper
with light feet.

Was I crazy before you lied?
I listen as you paint this picture of me
lies drawn to perfection
gaslit portrayals of what used to be
broken theories of my fragile existence...
but I remember who I was
before you lied.

I was not crazy.

Sleepless nights lead to idle hands
itching to scroll through your accounts
checking for any sign of neglect
displeasure or unhappiness...

Your smile turns me off
and I go back numb...
for I was fueled by the promise of karma
which is taking its own sweet time
bringing you to your knees.

MEMORIES THAT HAUNT ME

I remember the first time you raised your voice
and then your fist
and I watched the holes in the wall
become a visual reminder
of what you could do
if I pushed you too far.

I remember the moment
I stopped being afraid
the feel of the small knife in my hand
ready to defend myself
at a moment's notice.

This is not love.

In the darkest moments
my brain romanticizes what we had
and I forget, for a moment,
the nights that I cried while you slept.
I forget the loneliness,
the way I begged God to give me
the strength to leave you,
I forget how each day was a test
and I became the master of walking on
eggshells... just to please you
and keep you calm.

For a moment, I forget
how miserable
I truly was.

The scariest part of it all
is that in our bed
I whispered my fears to you
and confided in you
about the demons I battled...
and you took in everything I told you
and put me through the exact hell
that you promised to rescue me from.

We fought to stay together
you swore you couldn't live without me
but look at you... flourishing without my love
thriving in a way that only you know how...
and I am alone,
a weeping willow,
unloved and abandoned.

Peace is a word I hide from
because I have never truly seen it
and at this moment,
I am unsure that it exists.

Relationships were not meant to bring us peace
that much I do know...
and while a person's love may feel like a refuge
from the storms that life may bring...

remember that we come into this world
crying and afraid
and many of us
will leave that way as well.

I was never big on affection
and you smothered me with sweet kisses
and hugs that made me melt
sweet pinches to my stomach
that made me squeal with laughter...

The absence of affection
was a far greater loss
than anything I had experienced before.

My touch-deprived body longs for your caress
and my heart breaks at this yearning
that once never existed.

Target practice...
that is what loving you felt like,
at times,
your careless aim toward my unyielding heart
cruel jabs that I took with a grain of salt
and I remember thinking,
so, this is love...
the up and down of it all
seemed exciting
so long ago.

At some point,
I had to admit that deep down
I knew who you were
and what you were all about.

I chose to still go along for the ride...
thinking that a beautiful heartbreak was better
than never loving you at all.

You made me eat those words
bitter in my mouth
and I still have the taste of regret
on my tongue.

You loved making me smile
by meeting my material demands
keeping me
sparkly and shiny
on the outside
for the world to see.

This... you excelled in.

The rest...
well, the lack of nourishment
almost caused decay
but I think I caught the infection...
just in time.

The heart wants what it wants
like a toddler
untrustworthy and greedy
and only focused on
instant gratification.

I ignore my heart
and her feeble attempts to convince me
that you are the one
that I should love.

Some lessons are learned
the hard way.

Tired dolls
break easily under pressure
the weight of you
lingers…
it blazes my soul
an internal hell
the sounds of your anger
a gentle lullaby
that lulls my demons
to sleep.

Digging deep
holding my soul accountable
because these bodies are adding up…
and you're still gone
but the memory of you makes me ache
and I am convinced that
toxic kisses and empty hugs
are better than nothing at all.

Texting me at 2 am
when I know you're in bed with her
is such a slap in the face...
and yet, I respond,
hungrily,
anxious to see what is keeping you awake,
and relishing in the idea that maybe,
it's because you miss me.

Is that what's keeping you up
at night?

You liked my nails pink
always the softest shades
because they reminded you of the sunsets
when the sun-kissed sky melted into dusk
and we kissed in your car,
softly...
your lips imprinted with my soul
and now I hate pink,
on my nails or in the sky,
because it makes my eyes burn
with tears.

You left a note inside my pillowcase...
it slipped out one night
as I changed my bedding,
and curiously, I unfolded the paper
taking in your scratchy jolted writing
and my heart detached from my soul
so that each one could break
in their own way.

Our song plays in the background
and suddenly I am in a puddle of confusion
because surely, I will not fold
for lyrics and a hook… right?
And yet, watch as my knees buckle
my breath gets caught in my throat
and those damned tears… they threaten to fall
and expose me as a phony pretending to be healed.

You taught me that closed mouths
get rewarded with soft touches
and gentle smiles...

Closed mouths don't get pushed or punched
and pretty girls don't need to have an opinion
about everything, right?

Closed mouths don't get punished
with the silent treatment and the late nights out
wondering when or if you will come home...

If only I had learned when to shut my mouth.

Stubborn girls die alone.

I think about that often...

I lit two candles tied with a string
in an attempt
to break out trauma bond
and I watched as my candle held that string
to the very end...

Its fiery death was overshadowed
by my loud gasps of pain
as I understood, at that moment,
that I was the only one in this fever dream
that was unwilling to truly
let go.

TOXIC AND MESSY

Double lives…
smiling with my girls
bragging about how long you've been blocked
dancing in the club
twerking to the bass that makes me ache
in the places that miss you the most
because
once I get home
I text you and wait for the response
and if you offer to pull up
I'm ready
tripping over my feet and my bruised ego
to open the door
open my heart
and open my legs…

for you.

You don't post me
I stalk your pages to see who is getting
the hearts that I crave so much but
you do not post me
because you like your privacy and
I respect your boundaries
but my new man will post me
and I watch as you leave a heart on his post
and just like that...
I'm overanalyzing things
and missing you
and wondering if the grass
is truly greener
over here.

Your phone reveals who you really are
but you refuse to let me look
and I wish to God I had allowed you to cheat
in peace...
because I snuck and looked
and read every text
every word to her, and her, and her...
these silly girls with their gorgeous smiles
and quick replies...
and I couldn't leave you alone.
I refused to leave you alone.
I was here first
and these girls are temporary toys
and we both know
time can heal these wounds...
right?

My girls are tired of hearing me cry on the phone
and yet
I just cannot leave you alone
but I am trying...
do we get points for trying?
You are an addiction that I cannot shake
I feel the withdrawal in my bones
the wear and tear on my heart
and I'm stuck on stupid
because I just know in my soul...
once I give up on you
then some other girl will get the love
I deserved.

Making you cry seems like an unachievable feat
but I want it
I need to see your tear-stained pillowcase
I need to hear you scream out in agony
at the thought of losing me
because I have afforded you too many
sleepless nights
filled with hollowed-out cries
to the gods who will listen
to a girl who has lost love
once again…

Remember when we swore,
we would never
act like this over a man
we swore we were too smart
too independent
and way too secure in our self-awareness
to be like those other girls...

Well, we lied.
We lied.

Sometimes... in the corner of my mind
I wish I had the balls to kill you
rather than let another woman
learn how you like to be pleased
and the thought of her making you smile
or the idea you are doing everything I begged for
without effort because,
of course,
she deserves it...

the very thought of it drives me mad.

I cleaned up my act for you...
cut all my other guys off,
prayed to be a better woman,
and I gave you the very essence of who I am
without the filters or blinders...
and you fumbled me
anyway.

What was the goddamn point?

Have my baby, he whispers
soft wet kisses that line my face
promises made as you learn how
to navigate my designs
from the inside out...

Have my baby, he demands
time after time
I fall victim to the lies because they taste like
honey
against my greedy mouth as I gorge on the
fiction
of our love story.

Why did I have his baby, I whisper
all alone and depressed.

Another walking statistic.

We refuse to let each other go
and we creep behind the backs of way too
many innocent relationships...
Messy love that seeps around the edges of cruelty...
our partners don't deserve this but
we are addicted to the trauma bonds
that keep us coming back
time and time
again.

One minute you are inside my thoughts
inside of me
intimate and deep...
and now we barely speak.

You are a stranger to me,
cold and unbothered,
and I hate the very thought of you...

but,
I can readily admit that there is a flurry
of excitement
every time we speak in circles
about never getting back
together.

Gracious.
I was doing charity work,
loving you from the bottom up,
and putting value on your potential
because I was determined to build you up...
Foolish, I was, to think you would be thankful
and appreciate me
when you never fully learned to appreciate yourself.
I cannot save you from drowning
in the sea of mediocrity
any longer.

You are... your father's son.

I know you have a girl now
but deep down
my conscience has left the building...
selfishly, I need you here with me
and these small stolen moments
are my favorite.

Her spot is safe for now...
I do not want to be your woman anymore.
But I just can't let you go...
not yet, anyway.

Blocked messages,
left on read,
we went from
"Meant to be"
to
"Never call my phone again"
and all I can think is...

maybe this is just how our love story goes.

He will come back to me.
Of this, I'm sure.

I have his heart in the palm of my hand
and he proves it by engaging in this silly drama
with me when he could easily
cut me off and move on...

and yet,
here we are, again.

I want to call your wife
and ask her to accept the truth
which is, I cannot do without you...
And I won't do without you.

Every time you text, I will answer
and when you pull up,
I'm shaved, showered, and ready
because when I moaned that it was yours...
I meant that.

We are distant sister wives for now,
and she can keep her ignorant bliss
and I will keep the part of you
that remains
mine.

If you truly wanted her
you wouldn't stay up late to text me
or call me when she goes to work
and send me heart-eyed messages that swear
your allegiance to me...
as long as we don't get caught.

Don't worry love,
I'm no fool.

I know we are on quicksand
and that you would quickly release me
to avoid drowning.

You cried when you heard I was engaged
and my heart whispered that those tears
would ignite a false sense of security in me...
but I refused to listen.

I went to you and risked it all
for one more night...
of empty promises and lies
and more time in your embrace,
fiery kisses and passion,
and then the usual emptiness that follows
our encounters.

AFTERWORD

As I read through my poetry collection, I Thought I Missed Him, I can't help but be drawn in by the raw emotion and vulnerability on display. These poems delve deep into the complex and often toxic emotions that can arise when a relationship comes to an end.

It's important to note that while some of my poems may touch on toxic behavior, this collection should not be viewed as promoting such behavior. Instead, my intention is to explore the various ways we deal with the pain of a relationship ending, even when those ways may not always be healthy or productive.

Ultimately, I Thought I Missed Him is a testament to the power of poetry to capture the messy, complicated, and often contradictory emotions that we experience in the aftermath of a breakup. It's a reminder that healing is a journey and that sometimes, the first step towards moving forward is acknowledging our pain, no matter how ugly or uncomfortable it may be.

I wish you all healing and love.

ACKNOWLEDGEMENT

I would like to thank my loyal readers and new readers... thank you for taking a chance on me! I would love to interact and engage with you via email at teachermom0215@gmail.com or on my social media platforms @AuthorDianaTownsend. Thank you for proving to the world that poetry is not dying nor dead... it is alive in us.

Please take a few moments to write a review. Reviews help indie authors, like myself, stay in rotation!

Thank you!

BOOKS BY THIS AUTHOR

Iced Coffee And Depression

Iced Coffee and Depression is a raw and poignant collection of poetry that explores the complexities of depression and anxiety, the highs and lows of love and heartbreak, and the journey toward healing. Through vivid imagery and candid language, Diana Townsend takes the reader on an emotional journey that is both relatable and deeply personal. Whether you're struggling with mental health issues, recovering from a broken heart, or simply looking for a deeper understanding of the human experience, this book is for you. With its powerful and honest voice, Iced Coffee and Depression is a reminder that you are not alone in your struggles, and that healing is possible.

Things We Can't Escape: Poetry For The Brokenhearted

"Things We Can't Escape: Poetry for the

Brokenhearted" is a collection of raw and powerful poetry that delves into the depths of heartbreak and pain. Diana Townsend takes the reader on a journey through the complexities of grief and loss, exploring the emotions that come with being brokenhearted. The verses in this book are evocative and moving, leaving the reader with a deeper understanding of the human experience and the things we cannot escape. This book is a must-read for anyone who has ever had their heart broken

Black Girl Evolving

Black Girl Evolving is a powerful and evocative poetry collection that delves into the complexities of the black community, mental health, and the vital role of black women in society. Diana Townsend's vivid and raw voice, speaks to the struggles and triumphs of being a black woman in today's world. Each poem is a reflection of the personal experiences of the author, and the universal experiences of the black community. Through the lens of mental health, Townsend explores the resilience and the beauty of black women, and the importance of self-care, self-love, and self-empowerment. Black Girl Evolving is a must-read for anyone looking to gain a deeper understanding of the black community and the impact of mental health on black women. This powerful collection of poetry is an essential and inspiring read for anyone looking to understand the beauty, strength, and resilience of the black woman.

Black Girl Evolving Ii: Journey To Softness

Black Girl Evolving II: Journey to Softness is a powerful and moving collection of poems that delves deep into the experiences of black women, exploring themes of childhood innocence and trauma, young adulthood, and the journey towards softness and self-love.

From the very first poem, the reader is drawn into a world of raw emotion and vulnerability, as the author shares her own personal experiences of growing up as a black girl in a world that often feels hostile and unwelcoming. Through her poetry, she captures the complexity of these experiences, weaving together moments of joy, pain, and resilience in a way that is both intimate and universal.

Ultimately, Black Girl Evolving II: Journey to Softness is a testament to the resilience and softness of black women everywhere. Through her poetry, the author invites us to share her journey toward self-love and acceptance, reminding us that even in the darkest times, there is always the possibility of growth and transformation.

Love Is For The Dreamers

Love is for the Dreamers is a breathtaking collection of poetry that celebrates the magic and wonder of love. Written with passion and heart, these poems capture the essence of falling and staying in love, reminding us of its beauty and power. With its sweet and romantic tone, this book will sweep you off your feet and transport you to a world where anything is possible. Whether you're a hopeless romantic or simply seeking inspiration, Love is for the Dreamers is a must-read for anyone who believes in the power of love.

Made in the USA
Columbia, SC
18 July 2023